Savvy

CHOICE WORDS!

BY REBECCA LANGSTON-GEORGE

A CRASH COURSE IN *Language Arts*

T0081028

Consultant:
Susan E. Fello, EdD
Middle Level Education Coordinator
Indiana University of Pennsylvania
Indiana, Pennsylvania

CAPSTONE PRESS
a capstone imprint

Savvy Books are published by Capstone Press,
1710 Roe Crest Drive, North Mankato, Minnesota 56003
www.capstonepub.com

Library of Congress Cataloging-in-Publication Data
Langston-George, Rebecca.
  Choice words! : a crash course in language arts / by Rebecca Langston-George.
    pages cm. — (Crash course)
  Includes index.
  Summary: "Simplifies junior high English in engaging and conversational language and
offers examples and activities to show readers how the topics tie in to real life"—Provided by
publisher.
  ISBN 978-1-4914-0773-8 (library binding)
  ISBN 978-1-4914-0781-3 (paperback)
  ISBN 978-1-4914-0777-6 (eBook pdf)
  1. Language arts (Middle school) 2. English language—Study and teaching (Middle school) I.
Title.
  LB1631.L224 2014
  428.0071'2—dc23

                              2014012076

Editorial Credits
Abby Colich, editor; Lori Bye, designer; Gina Kammer, media researcher;
Kathy McColley, production specialist

Photo Credits
Shutterstock: Aaron Amat, 55, Africa Studio, 8, 34, (drape) 38, 45, Aigars Reinholds, 43, Al
Mueller, 36, alekso94 (girl with book), 29, Andre Jabali (equalizer background), 11, Antonio
Guillem, 53, Ariwasabi, 10, Aspen Photo, 22, AYakovlev, 7, 16, B Calkins (top), 57, bitt24, 50,
David Acosta Allely, 44, Elena Schweitzer, 42, Feng Yu, 12, glenda, 58, Goodluz, 52, Gray Ng
(girl), 9, back cover, Hugo Felix, 49, Hurst Photo, 14, iko, 23, Ivonne Wierink (bottom), 57,
Jill Chen (girl with confetti), 39, jmcdermottillo (pop art style faces), cover and throughout,
Julia Ivantsova (pencil), 13, Kazarlenya, 35, Kitch Bain, 41, Kjpargeter, 30, Kudryashka, (hand-
drawn colorful wave pattern), throughout, LanKS (open book), 29, Luba V Nel (girl), 18, Lucky
Business, 15, Maks Narodenko, 51, markos86, 20, Mikado767 (equalizer background), 18,
NinaMalyna, 40, Odua Images, 5, 37, Olga Danylenko, 32, Oligo (WOW!), 11, OLJ Studio, 59,
back cover, Paul Matthew Photography (student), 13, Pressmaster, 25, Ramona Kaulitzki, 21,
Rido, 48, Rob Marmion (two girls), 39, Sally Scott, 46, sergo iv (bottle), 38, Spectral-Design, 27,
stockyimages (rhythm design), 9, underworld, 54, Vezzani Photography, 56, wavebreakmedia
(two girls), 29

Design elements: Shutterstock

Printed in the United States of America in Stevens Point, Wisconsin.
032014   008092WZF14

Table of Contents

THE LOWDOWN ON LANGUAGE ARTS.................................. 4

CHAPTER 1
GRAMMAR IS THE RHYTHM OF LANGUAGE........................ 6

CHAPTER 2
LITERATURE IS ALL ABOUT THE DRAMA......................... 22

CHAPTER 3
READING INFORMATIONAL TEXT TO PLAN YOUR NEXT PARTY...34

CHAPTER 4
WRITING IS AS EASY AS FOLLOWING A RECIPE 44

GLOSSARY 62
READ MORE 63
INTERNET SITES... 63
INDEX... 64

THE LOWDOWN ON LANGUAGE ARTS

Ever feel like nobody is listening when you talk? Having trouble getting your parents to see your side of an argument? Believe it or not, Language Arts class can help. Surprised? Language is all about communicating. Speaking and writing are ways you communicate, and listening and reading are how we understand communication.

By learning how communication works, you'll be able to speak your mind effectively and confidently. After all, you're full of opinions and important ideas. You deserve to be heard. People are more likely to pay attention if you communicate well.

You might be thinking that grammar is a bunch of boring rules. Or that literature is difficult to understand and that writing is hard. But if you can learn the latest dance craze, then you can understand grammar rules. If you can listen to your best friend's boy problems, you can understand literature. If you can plan a party or follow a recipe, then you'll be able to research and write without a problem.

How to Use This Book

This book is designed so you can read the chapters in any order you like. If you have a grammar, literature, informational reading, or writing assignment, you can find that section quickly and get the information you need. Each chapter has a fun activity to try out each new skill. You'll find the answers in the back.

CHAPTER 1

GRAMMAR IS THE RHYTHM OF LANGUAGE

Have you ever been to one of those dances where all the girls sit on one side of the gymnasium and all the boys sit on the other? Awkward! Until finally, a couple of bold people get up and start dancing. Eventually, other people join them. But there are always a few wallflowers who can't find the courage to get on the dance floor.

The same is true when it comes to grammar. The teacher asks a grammar question, and everyone looks down at the floor. Nobody wants to speak up. But once you get the hang of it, grammar is actually a lot like dancing. How? Grammar is the rhythm of the language. It's the beat. Once you understand the rhythm of the language, your writing and speaking are going to rock!

WARM-UP TIME

Think of it this way. Dances are made up of small steps or parts that are linked together. So is language. In language we call these parts of speech. There are only eight parts of speech.

The Eight Parts of Speech:

noun	adjective
pronoun	preposition
verb	conjunction
adverb	interjection

To dance you have to do a minimum of two basic moves. You have to move your feet and arms. To create a sentence, you have to have two parts—the subject and the predicate. The subject usually comes first. It's either a noun—a person, place, thing or idea. Or it's a pronoun—a word that takes the place of a noun (like using I instead of your name). The predicate usually comes after the subject. The predicate is the verb (the action word or linking word) as well as everything that follows the verb. Here's an example:

The boy / likes to dance.
subject / predicate

ADD SOME STYLE

Once you get your feet and arms moving, you're going to want to add some style. You might turn quickly or slowly. When you add descriptions to your verbs, or action words, such as "quickly" or "slowly," you're adding an adverb. This is a word that describes how the action is done. Maybe you snap the fingers on your right hand. Adding a description such as "right" to the noun "hand" is using an adjective.

Just like you turn in different directions as you dance, your sentences might need some direction too. Words that add direction are called prepositions.

QUICK TIP

The word "position" inside preposition will help you remember what it does.

There are just two more parts of speech. Conjunctions connect things. There are seven conjunctions—but, or, yet, for, and, nor, so.

Wow! The last part of speech is the interjection. Interjections (like the word "Wow!") show emotion. Think of interjections as the attitude you show when you dance.

QUICK TIP

You can remember the seven conjunctions with the acronym BOYFANS.

POP QUIZ

Adjectives describe _____, and adverbs describe _____.

MASTER THESE
Two Moves

Now that you have the eight basic dance steps mastered, it's time to put them together to create some dances. A dance is just a set of moves connected together. When you connect words together, you get clauses (groups of words) that create sentences. Good news! In English there are only two basic types of clauses and four different types of sentences. Four! That's it.

The two types of clauses are independent and subordinate. An independent clause has a subject, verb, and complete thought. It could stand alone as a sentence because it's strong and independent. Think of a weight lifter who doesn't need any help to get the job done. Take a look at these two examples:

Brittany has a new blue backpack.
My dog jumped over the fence.

QUICK TIP
Independent clauses can stand alone as sentences.

The other type of clause is subordinate. A subordinate clause is missing something. It might lack the subject, verb, or complete thought. It has to lean on the strong independent clause to make a complete sentence because it can't pull its own weight. When you write a subordinate clause as if it were an independent clause, it's called a fragment. A fragment is a piece of a sentence, but it can't stand on its own. Avoid fragments such as the examples below. It'll keep your teacher happy.

Because I didn't finish my homework. Over by the drinking fountain.

SHALL WE *Dance?*

Let's mix some independent clauses and subordinate clauses to make sentences. The easiest one to start with is a simple sentence. It really is simple because it's just one independent clause on its own. Here is an example:

The bus is late today.

If you combine two independent clauses, you create a compound sentence. Compound sentences contain either a comma followed by a conjunction (remember BOYFANS) or a semicolon. Here are two examples:

I want to go to the movies, but I don't have enough money.

The monkey got out of its cage; it's throwing bananas everywhere!

Now it's time to invite the subordinate clause to the dance. When you combine an independent clause with a subordinate clause you create a complex sentence. Here's an example:

Because I didn't finish my homework, I'm worried about the test today.

Notice that if you switched the clauses around you would leave out the comma like this:

I'm worried about the test today because I didn't finish my homework.

QUICK TIP

One independent clause makes a simple sentence. Two independent clauses make a compound sentence.

14

QUICK TIP

If your subordinate clause comes first, it's followed with a comma. If it comes last, it doesn't need a comma.

Now for the dancing queen diva of all sentences—the compound-complex sentence. It's got at least three clauses with a combination of independent clauses and subordinate clauses. Drum roll please ...

Grammar may seem scary, but you can do it because it's just like dancing.

Do you see the three clauses?

Grammar may seem scary
(independent clause)

you can do it
(independent clause)

because it's just like dancing.
(subordinate clause)

POP QUIZ

I don't know about you, but I feel like dancing!

What kind of sentence is this?

Bonus Point

What is the conjunction in the above example?

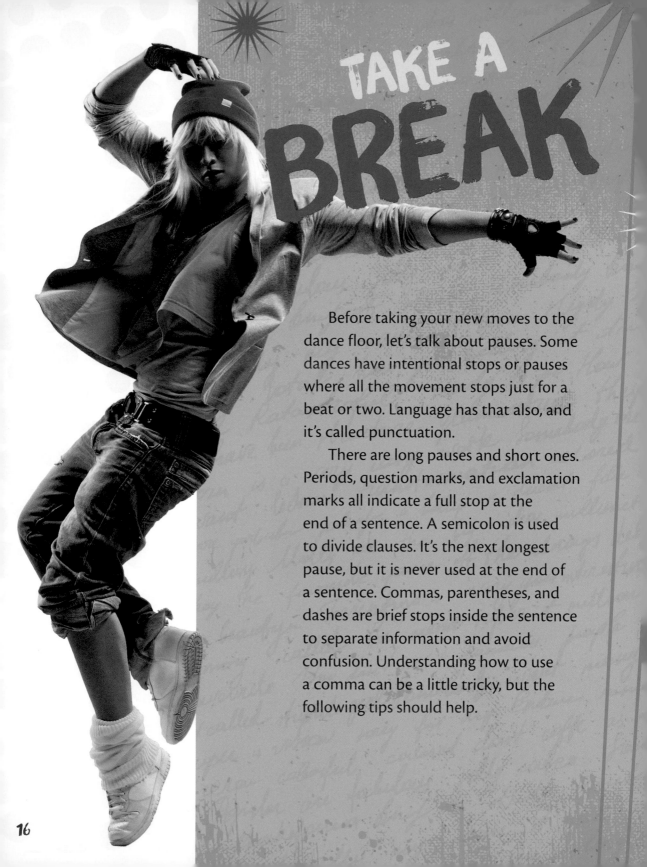

TAKE A
BREAK

Before taking your new moves to the dance floor, let's talk about pauses. Some dances have intentional stops or pauses where all the movement stops just for a beat or two. Language has that also, and it's called punctuation.

There are long pauses and short ones. Periods, question marks, and exclamation marks all indicate a full stop at the end of a sentence. A semicolon is used to divide clauses. It's the next longest pause, but it is never used at the end of a sentence. Commas, parentheses, and dashes are brief stops inside the sentence to separate information and avoid confusion. Understanding how to use a comma can be a little tricky, but the following tips should help.

Set off the name of someone you're addressing or the words "yes" and "no" when you use them at the beginning of a sentence:

Nigel, please turn off the radio.

No, that's not my jacket.

Separate the speech tag from the quotation with a comma:

Hunter asked, "Would you like to dance?"

Place a comma before a coordinating conjunction in a compound sentence:

My favorite song is on, but I'm too tired to sing along.

Insert a comma when listing items in a series:

The dance studio offers tap, ballet, and hip-hop classes.

Another punctuation mark is the apostrophe. It is used to replace a missing letter in contractions or to show possession.

Contractions:

don't
isn't

Possessives:

Sophia's purse
Joel's lunch box

Plural possessives:

the kids' playground
the girls' locker room

QUICK TIP

When a group owns or possesses something, it's called a plural possessive. In this case the playground belongs to all of the kids. When you write a plural possessive word, be sure to place an apostrophe after the letter s.

Finally, if you need to write dialogue or quote what someone else said, you use quotation marks. These come in a pair of marks at the beginning and a pair of marks at the end. Because they come in pairs, and you use them when a character talks, think of them as a couple who talks to one another.

"Why don't you like to dance?" asked Bree. Aidan replied, "I've got two left feet."

If you quote what Bree said, you'd have a quotation inside a quotation. To avoid confusion, use single quotations around a quote inside a quote.

Aidan said, "Can you believe that, Bree? When I told her I have two left feet, she said, 'It must be hard to find shoes.'"

The Rhythm of Language

Don't be a grammar wallflower. Just like learning the newest dance move takes some practice, so does learning grammar. You can be the queen of the language dance floor, speaking, writing, and proclaiming what's on your mind by remembering a few simple steps. Subjects and predicates are the basic moves every sentence needs. Add style with descriptive adjectives and adverbs. Mix it up by using all four types of sentences. Learn the rhythm of language, and you'll take center stage.

Real-World Language Arts

Ever heard the saying "First impressions count"? The way you communicate makes an impression on people. Whether you're filling out a job application, giving an oral report, or preparing a slide show, the way you communicate sends a message about who you are. Teachers, colleges, and employers make quick judgments about your education, ability, and responsibility based on how well you speak and write.

Imagine you're starting your own business. You've learned your trade, invested a lot of money, and sent out advertising. You hand out your newly designed business cards proclaiming, "We go the extra mile to serve our customer's." Uh-oh! Can customers really trust a company that can't proofread its own business cards?

No matter what career you pursue, it will involve communication. Learning the basics of grammar will help you communicate effectively and confidently.

LEARN THE LANGUAGE

Decide if the following sentences are simple, compound, complex, or compound-complex.

1. _____ Everyone knows dancing is fun.

2. _____ I chose this dress because the rhinestones will sparkle on the dance floor.

3. _____ Although Brittany says she has two left feet, she was on the dance floor for every dance, and everyone said she was a dancing diva.

4. _____ We were tired after dancing, so we took a break.

Now try some writing of your own. Create four different sentences, making each one harder than the last using all the clauses and sentence types you know.

5. First, create a simple sentence. Use one independent clause.

6. Next, hook two independent clauses together to make a compound sentence.

7. Now bring in one independent clause and one subordinate clause to create a complex sentence.
Bonus points: Can you write your sentence two different ways. First, start with the subordinate clause, then try it with the subordinate clause at the end. Remember which one needs a comma.

8. Time to put all your skills to the test! This is where we see if you're a real pro. Write the most difficult sentence of all, the compound-complex sentence. (Hint: like the name says it's just a combination of a compound sentence and a complex sentence.)

CHAPTER 2

LITERATURE IS ALL ABOUT THE DRAMA

Your best friend calls to tell you that her crush just asked another girl to the dance. You settle back against the bed pillows and listen, knowing you're about to get an earful of drama. Being a great friend, you know that your BFF is counting on you to understand. So what do you do? You listen as she talks, and you try to figure out what happened.

In literature, or a fictional story, this is called the plot. Plot is the sequence of events that happen in the story. Those events often lead to a conflict, or problem, for the main character. In your friend's case, the conflict is the fact that her crush asked another girl to the dance.

GET TO THE POINT

As you listen to your friend, you try to figure out what caused the conflict. Why did her crush ask out another girl? Depending on who you ask, you'll probably get different answers. People interpret events differently based on what they know and how it affects them. That's called the point of view.

Your friend's crush may have one answer to what caused the conflict. (I didn't know you liked me! You're making a big deal out of nothing.) Your best friend will have another answer. (How can he be so mean to me? He's hurting my feelings.) When a character tells about events he or she experienced, that's called first-person point of view. One clue to first-person point of view is the use of personal pronouns such as I, me, my, mine, we, or us.

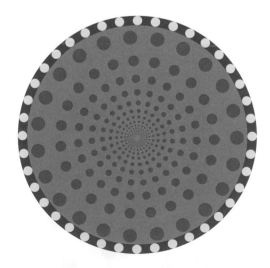

Do you see some first-person pronouns in their explanations? But the two people involved in the conflict aren't the only ones who have points of view. Let's say other friends overheard the boy asking out the other girl. When witnesses describe what they saw happen, it's called third-person point of view. (Your friend's crush saw her helping another boy with his math homework before he asked another girl to the dance.) One way to spot third-person point of view is the use of third-person pronouns such as she, he, her, him, they, and them.

QUICK TIP

Point of view can usually be determined by looking at the pronouns.

READ BETWEEN THE LINES

So far you have a plot with a conflict and three points of view on what happened. But you aren't any closer to untangling why the conflict happened. What's a best friend to do? Try reading between the lines. Is there anything that you should look at more closely?

Let's take another look at that comment from the person in the lunch line.

"Your friend's crush saw her helping another boy with his math homework before he asked another girl to the dance." Hmmm. Notice how the crush acted right after seeing your friend with another boy. What does that tell you? Look at the crush's comments too.

"I didn't know you liked me." He didn't know your friend liked him. Could there be a misunderstanding? When you add your common sense to what you hear or read, you infer.

Rereading key points and thinking about them can help you make inferences. Sometimes people don't come right out and say what they think. Authors do the same thing. They leave room for you to think and figure things out for yourself.

POP QUIZ

Look at the above sentence again. "Sometimes people don't come right out and say what they think." Is that first- or third-person point of view?

LEARN YOUR LESSON

You and your friend have now figured out that the conflict was caused by a misunderstanding. Maybe your friend can patch things up with her crush. In a story that's called the resolution. Drama over, right? Not so fast. What's to keep your friend from getting upset again in the future? Did she learn any lessons from what happened?

The life lesson a character learns in a story is called the theme. To figure out the theme, always look at the root of the conflict. Once you know the lesson that the character learns from going through the conflict, you've arrived at the theme.

QUICK TIP

Notice how the word "solution" is inside resolution? That's because the resolution is when the conflict gets solved.

What a Character!

Whew! You've talked your friend through the crush crisis. Once you hang up the phone, you wonder if your friend could have avoided the crisis. Maybe he's not the right guy for your friend. You think back about how he behaves, the things he's said, and what other people have said about him. In literature the description of a character's personality is called characterization. Look at what a character says, how he or she behaves, and what other characters say or do around that character to determine characterization.

DON'T TAKE THIS
Literally

After all your hard work on the phone with your friend, you decide to take a break. You turn on some music and listen to one of your favorite songs.

Tough as an iron nail,

She's anything but frail.

Unafraid to speak her mind,

She's gold and steel combined.

Music, like literature, takes some thinking to understand. Notice the interesting way the lyrics describe the character in the song. "Tough as an iron nail" is a simile, a comparison of two unlike things using the words "like" or "as."

When the song says, "She's gold and steel combined," the songwriter is using a metaphor. A metaphor is a comparison of two unlike things, saying one thing is another. Wait a minute! Doesn't that sound like a simile? A metaphor compares things without using "like" or "as." The writer also uses an idiom, a poetic description in which the words don't add up to the literal meaning. "Speak her mind" is an idiom for expressing yourself.

QUICK TIP

The key to telling a simile and metaphor apart is the use of the word "like" or "as." A comparison using "like" or "as" is a simile.

Real-World Language Arts: Screenwriter

Authors aren't the only people who make a living by telling stories. Screenwriters also write stories, but their stories are called scripts. They are produced into movies or TV shows instead of books.

Scripts list the dialogue, or speaking parts, for the actors as well as directions on how they should act. Camera angles and set descriptions may also be included. Just like authors, screenwriters use plot, conflict, resolution, and theme to create their scripts.

Most screenwriters do freelance work, which means they work for themselves. They pitch, or try to sell, their work to TV networks or movie studios. Some go to college to earn a degree in screenwriting.

DRAMA iN THE
Classroom

The next time the teacher asks you to tell what happened in the story, just pull out your BFF listening tools. Let's say you are assigned to write a report on *The Secret Garden* or *The Little Prince*. Writing about your favorite part or telling whether you liked the story is not going to make the grade.

Show your teacher you really paid attention and analyzed the story. Start out by introducing the characters. Tell the events that happen in the plot. Describe the conflict and resolution. End with a bang by telling the theme. Then sit back and get ready to collect your hard-earned A+.

LEARN THE LANGUAGE

1. TV shows and movies follow the same patterns as books. They are visual stories. The next time you watch a fictional TV show (not a reality or nature show) have a piece of paper and a pen handy. See if you can write down the sequence of events in the plot. Write down what the conflict and resolution are and name the theme by the end.

2. Here's an easy way to analyze the main character in a book. Try it the next time you read a piece of fiction. Fold a piece of paper in thirds. Label three columns:

- how the character behaves
- what the character says
- what others say about the character

Jot down notes in each column as you read. When you've got several notes in each column, see if you can use the notes to come up with three words to describe the main character.

3. Similes and metaphors are great ways to spice up your writing. Songs are full of them. The next time you listen to your favorite song, see how many you can find. Try your hand at creating a few yourself using the examples below to get you started.

Similes

The bulldog was as mean as _____ .

Her eyes were blue like _____ .

The newborn chick was as soft as _____ .

Metaphors

He's a _____ when he plays football.

My little sister turns into a _____ when she doesn't get her way.

My neighbor is usually cranky, but when she talks to her new kitten she becomes a _____ .

CHAPTER 3

READING INFORMATIONAL TEXT TO PLAN YOUR NEXT PARTY

You've been begging your parents to let you throw a party. You want a big bash with music, food, and decorations. Your parents agree but with one condition. You have to plan the party yourself and stay within a budget they set. Great news! Ready to start planning? Knowing how to read and interpret informational texts will help you plan the best party ever.

Reading informational texts such as science textbooks, newspapers, and product reviews is very different from reading literature. Instead of reading to enjoy the plot, you are reading nonfiction to gain information on a specific topic.

Gather Evidence

In order to plan, you'll need some information. You search the Internet because you want to rent a karaoke machine. You want to compare prices, but you also want to make sure you get a quality machine that will keep the party fun and happening. One brand advertises that it has the best karaoke machine on the planet. Whoa! Best on the planet? That's a pretty big claim. How can it back that up?

Good readers always look for evidence that supports a claim or main idea. Quotations, citations, and statistics are good evidence. Unfortunately, that company doesn't offer any evidence to back up its claim. Maybe you better look at another website. The Cool Times Karaoke Machine advertises its battery runs for six hours without needing to recharge. The label includes a graph comparing its battery life to other karaoke machines. There's a sticker advertising it's a *Consumer's Choice* product. Below that there is a review from *Consumer's Choice* magazine ranking the product with 4.5 stars out of 5. Clearly, Cool Times has some evidence to back up its claims.

QUICK TIP

Claims made without sufficient evidence to back them up cannot be trusted when reading or writing informational texts.

Get Informed

Next you visit some local sandwich shops to find out about food for the party. Each restaurant gives you a brochure. It lists information about the shop and has tables with prices. There are also some charts that list how much food they suggest for certain numbers of guests. Many of the brochures contain pictures with captions underneath.

Informational text often contains tables, charts, and graphs. There may be pictures with captions. Text that the writer wants you to pay special attention to may be bold or italicized. It's a good idea when reading this type of text to first scan the material, looking at pictures and captions. Also scan any tables and charts before reading.

QUICK TIP

Always read headings, captions, sidebars, and footnotes. These text features will help you better understand the information.

When looking at different catering brochures, you are doing a type of reading called compare and contrast. That means you're looking at how things are the same or different. Other types of nonfiction reading formats include chronology, cause and effect, how-to directions, and problem/solution.

Chronology is the timetable or order of events. You and your friends might come up with the order of the songs you want to karaoke during a two-hour party. That's a type of chronology. In informational texts, you can find chronology in timelines or in how the text is organized.

POP QUIZ

Fill in the blanks.

You read _____ to gain information.

You read _____ to enjoy the plot and be entertained.

Search for Solutions

Once you settle on the music and the food, you realize you have only $10 left for decorations. Uh-oh! That isn't going to buy much. You talk to your mom to see if she could add some money to your budget, but she won't budge. You tell her the $10 you have left won't even buy the purple tablecloth you want. Mom opens the linen closet and shows you a stack of old sheets. "Why don't you try one of these?" she asks. The sheets were once white but they've turned dingy gray over the years. You're about to say, "They'd be OK if they were purple," when you have a brainstorm. On the computer you type, "What to do with dingy sheets." You find a blog called the Savvy Homemaker.

Two weeks ago she wrote a blog about what to do with dingy sheets. She has two suggestions: you can bleach them back to white or dye them. Problem solved! The Savvy Homemaker just gave you a problem/solution format. With an inexpensive bottle of dye, you're able to transform one of the dingy sheets into a purple tablecloth. This blog entry served as a type of informational text.

COMMERCIAL BREAK

A great place to see a claim or position is a commercial. Next time you're watching TV, ask yourself what claim is the advertisement making. Then look for the evidence that's given to back up that claim. Ask yourself if the evidence is believable. Give the commercial a grade from A to F based on whether the evidence is convincing.

Look for Clues

Sometimes there are clues within text that help you figure out meaning. You're leafing through a magazine and see an ad for a photo booth. It looks like a blast. You type "make your own photo booth" into an Internet search engine. You find this do-it-yourself site that gives you the instructions you need.

Make Your Own Photo Booth

Making your own photo booth is easy. First, create a **backdrop** (1). Spray-painted cardboard, a large poster, or even a colored sheet will work. Next, gather some fun props. Funny glasses, vintage hats, plastic mustaches, and feather **boas** (2) are sure to please your guests. To make your own cardboard props, visit our website to download free **templates** (3) or patterns. Provide disposable cameras, and ask a friend to take the pictures. You can also encourage everyone to take **selfies** (4) by switching their cell phones to the self-picture mode.

Bonus Point

What type of informational text is the above?

Notice how the directions help you understand some of the terms. The four clues an author uses to help a reader understand vocabulary terms are context, definition, example, and restatement.

The photo booth directions use all four to hint at the meanings of the bolded words. See if you can match the bolded words in the photo booth paragraph to the four types of clues listed below.

_____ Context: A difficult word can be understood by the hints supplied by the other words around it.

_____ Definition: A difficult word may be understood by the definition following it.

_____ Example: Examples that follow the vocabulary word help you understand the word.

_____ Restatement: A synonym is given for a difficult word to help you understand its meaning.

Pat Yourself on the Back

Thanks to your savvy planning your party turned out great. Sure, it took some planning and thinking, but the end result was worth it. The same thing is true in the classroom.

Think of your next nonfiction reading assignment as if it were a party to plan. Read carefully to gather evidence and assess an author's claims.

Always look for proof that what the author says can be backed up with evidence. Pay attention to captions, graphics, and other text features so you don't miss any important information. When your teacher asks you to explain the nonfiction piece you read, just summarize the author's position or claim. Be sure to cite the evidence the author gives to back up the position or claim. When the good grades come rolling in, celebrate by throwing yourself a real party.

Party Games

Need more party ideas? First match each activity to the type of thinking it requires. Which is which? Your choices are:

compare and contrast
how-to directions
problem/solution

1. _____ Show a video that demonstrates a new dance craze and get everyone moving.

2. _____ Divide your guests into two teams. Give each team a camera and send them to separate rooms. Each team takes a picture of themselves, then takes the exact same picture again but switches 10 things around in the second picture. For example, in the second picture one person removes a hat, another frowns instead of smiles, and so on. Teams switch pictures and the first team to identify all 10 differences in the before and after pictures wins.

3. _____ Before the party starts, hide all the paper goods for the refreshment table. Place a giant "missing" sign above the cake and punch that says "Missing: cups, plates, napkins, and forks. Reward for the first person to find them." Give a riddle to the location of the missing goods. The first person to solve the riddle and find the goods wins a prize.

Real-World Language Arts: Editor

Pull any magazine article or book off of the shelf. You'll easily find the author's name, but it may surprise you to find out the author had some help. An editor verifies facts in a book or article, makes the corrections to grammar and punctuation, and makes sure the writing is interesting. He or she may arrange for artists to illustrate texts, as well as arrange for books and magazines to be marketed. In addition, editors negotiate contracts with writers and arrange for copyright permissions. If you're interested in becoming an editor, you'll want to get a degree in English. While you're in college, look for summer opportunities to intern at a publishing company

CHAPTER 4

WRITING IS AS EASY AS FOLLOWING A RECIPE

If you were asked to make a batch of brownies for the school bake sale, what would you do? You'd grab a bowl, some flour, and sugar and follow the directions. You could handle that, right?

What if you were asked to make an essay or a story? Not sure what you'd do? Writing is no different than baking brownies. All you have to do is follow a recipe.

There are three basic types of writing—argument, explanation, and narrative. Think of them as brownies, chocolate chip cookies, and chocolate cupcakes. These baked goods share some of the same ingredients and require some of the same tools. In the same way, all three types of writing share some similarities.

Whether you're baking brownies, chocolate chip cookies, or chocolate cupcakes, you're going to need the same basic ingredients—flour, sugar, eggs, and chocolate. The basic ingredients for all types of writing include answering the prompt, formal tone, transitions, and conclusions.

Basic Ingredients

Let's start with the obvious. A writer has to answer the prompt. Prompts are the directions that tell you what to do. To answer the prompt, always read the instructions carefully and completely when you're asked to do a writing assignment. Underline key words that tell you what to do. Just like all baked goods need a recipe, all writing needs a careful plan. Come up with a plan before you start writing so that your essay or story is organized. This is called prewriting.

Outline Template

Topic Sentence

I. Main idea
A. Explain, give details
B. Explain, give details
C. Explain, give details

II. Main idea
A. Explain, give details
B. Explain, give details
C. Explain, give details

III. Main idea
A. Explain, give details
B. Explain, give details
C. Explain, give details

Conclusion

A graphic organizer is a great way to plan your writing. An outline is another good way to plan your writing. Planning before you start takes a few extra minutes at the beginning but will save you time in the end.

You also will need to use a formal tone. The writing you do in school, college, and work is very different from the writing you do with friends such as texting or sending notes.

With your friends you can be casual, use abbreviations, and make jokes. But with school writing you want to make a great impression.

You need to be formal. Think of it as the difference between a picnic and a fancy dinner party. You communicate informally with your friends. When you write, you are more formal. Do not use abbreviations, slang, or text message lingo in formal writing.

Graphic Organizer Template

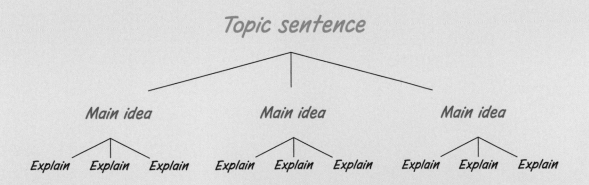

Topic sentence

Main idea   Main idea   Main idea

Explain Explain Explain   Explain Explain Explain   Explain Explain Explain

Conclusion

Transitions are another ingredient found in all types of writing. Transitions link ideas and paragraphs together. They often come at the beginning of paragraphs. Words such as "first," "next," "in addition," and "another" are all examples of transitions.

QUICK TIP

Transitions smooth the way between one idea and another.

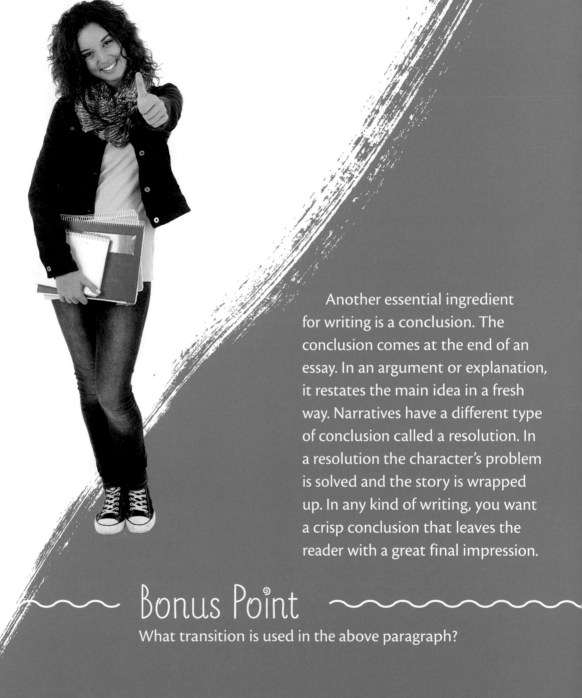

Another essential ingredient for writing is a conclusion. The conclusion comes at the end of an essay. In an argument or explanation, it restates the main idea in a fresh way. Narratives have a different type of conclusion called a resolution. In a resolution the character's problem is solved and the story is wrapped up. In any kind of writing, you want a crisp conclusion that leaves the reader with a great final impression.

Bonus Point

What transition is used in the above paragraph?

SPECIFIC *Recipes*

Here are three writing recipes that are guaranteed to please your teacher. Master the argument, explanation, and narrative, and you're sure to ace your language arts classes.

ARGUMENT

When writing an argument, also called an opinion, your job is to make a claim. Prove the claim using reasons, facts, and details. The following is an example of an argument prompt.

The principal is considering a proposal that would reward honor roll students. Honor roll students would be dismissed 20 minutes early for lunch and receive a 50-minute lunch period. Meanwhile, students who did not make honor roll would remain in class for study hall and receive the usual 30-minute lunch. Write a letter to the editor of the school newspaper stating your argument either for or against extended lunch for honor roll students.

QUICK TIP
Keep these two words in mind when writing an argument: "prove it."

First, decide how you feel about the issue. Are you for or against the proposal? Write your opinion as a topic sentence. A topic sentence is an answer to the topic or subject. For example, "A longer lunch period is a great way to reward honor students."

Now brainstorm of a couple of good reasons why your topic sentence is true:
• Good grades should be rewarded.
• Students not on the honor roll will work harder if there is a reward.
• Students already on honor roll will work hard to stay on it and continue getting rewarded.

QUICK TIP

A topic sentence comes at the top, and the top of the essay should tell the reader your answer to the topic.

Once you have your topic sentence and your reasons, you're ready to start prewriting and then writing. Be sure to back up your reasons with proof. You can prove things by giving examples, statistics, and evidence.

Or simply explain your reason more fully and with details. You should write a paragraph for each of your reasons.

To conclude your argument, restate the topic sentence in a fresh way and end with a memorable line.

POP QUIZ

The purpose of an argument is to see if you can make a _____ and _____ it.

Explanation

Let's say you're given the following prompt:

Your school is starting a new program called Career Cadets. Students chosen to be Career Cadets will be released from school one day each semester to receive supervised on-the-job training for a career of their choice. Only 20 students will be selected to participate. To apply you must write an essay explaining what career you would like to train for and why you believe that's the best career for you.

The hardest part of any essay is the beginning. Reread the prompt and find exactly what you're being asked to write about. Do you see it? "To apply you must write an essay telling what career you would like to train for and why you believe that's the best career for you." Now find the key words and use them to create a topic sentence. For example, do you want to be a nurse? Write this as your topic sentence, "I want to join Career Cadets and train to be a nurse."

Now you need to explain. The explanation usually answers a question. In this case the question is why you believe that's the best career for you. You'll need several paragraphs explaining why this is a good career choice for you. Use a transition before each reason. Be descriptive and answer the prompt completely. No one likes a cupcake with skimpy frosting. In the same way, teachers don't like essays that skimp on the details. Finish with a good conclusion and a memorable line.

NARRATIVE

The third type of writing your teacher might ask you to do is a narrative. A narrative is a fictional story. Narratives let you use your imagination. Look at the prompt below.

An old bottle with a stopper washes up on the beach. Inside is a genie waiting to grant one wish to whomever pulls out the stopper. Write a narrative telling what happens.

Narratives are very different from essays. You might be tempted to write something like this: "If I were granted a wish from a genie, I would choose a million dollars for three reasons."

Not so fast! That's an explanation, not a narrative. Narratives need a plot, a series of events that happen. Just like flour is necessary for cupcakes, conflict is a requirement for a narrative. When you pull the stopper on that bottle and choose your wish, it better cause some conflict. Be sure your narrative has a clear beginning, middle, and end with action, dialogue, and conflict.

Pay attention to the point of view you're asked to use. Describe things so the reader feels drawn in to the world you create. Use your imagination and have fun with your story.

QUICK TIP
Narrative is related to the word narrator, one who tells the story.

Narratives have special transitions that show the passage of time. Use transitions such as "later that day" or "by the time the sun set." Never use transitions such as "finally" or "in conclusion" in a narrative.

When writing what a character says (dialogue), be sure to start a new paragraph each time a character speaks.

"What is your dog doing under the couch?" asked Sasha.

"I think he's plotting," replied Anne.

"Wow!" exclaimed Sasha. "That's amazing. Our cat's never written a single sentence, much less a whole narrative."

A narrative's ending should resolve the conflict, or problem. It should be memorable. You can make your narrative's ending memorable by having your character do something unexpected.

Revising AND Presenting

When you bake a delicious cupcake and give it to a friend, you don't just slap it frosting first into her hand. That would make a very bad impression. Impressions count in writing too.

When you take a batch of cupcakes out of the oven, they are too hot to eat immediately. They need to cool, and then you take the time to frost them neatly. Do the same thing with your writing. Don't turn in a paper the minute you finish it. It needs some final touches.

It's a good idea to take a break when you finish writing. Come back to your writing when you've had a chance to rest a little bit and read through your writing. Look for errors. This is called editing. Have a friend read it for you as well. Look for ways to make it better by moving, deleting, or adding things. When you do this, you revise. After you've edited and revised, make a neat, clean copy of the writing to turn in to the teacher.

When a teacher pulls out an essay to grade, she forms a reaction before she even reads it. Is the handwriting neat? Or is the final document typed and printed on crisp, white paper? Does it have even margins all the way around it making it easy to read? Is it broken into paragraphs?

Did the writer include a heading with her name and other information? A pretty cupcake that's neatly frosted and placed in a decorative paper liner looks inviting to eat. Same thing goes when writing. A paper that looks neat and easy to read is more enjoyable than a messy one.

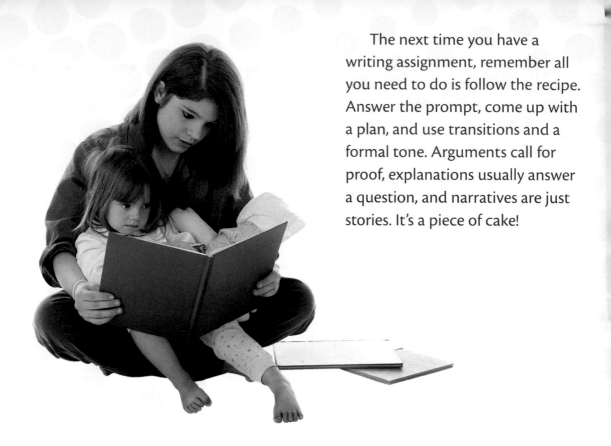

The next time you have a writing assignment, remember all you need to do is follow the recipe. Answer the prompt, come up with a plan, and use transitions and a formal tone. Arguments call for proof, explanations usually answer a question, and narratives are just stories. It's a piece of cake!

LEARN THE LANGUAGE

Use the following prompt to write a fictional narrative. When you're finished, use the rubric on page 61 to score your work.

You're babysitting your cousin on a dark, stormy night. Thunder roars above and lightning lights up the windows. To calm your cousin, you begin reading her a bedtime story. Suddenly there is a huge clap of thunder and the lights go out. When the lights come on, you realize you and your cousin are trapped inside the storybook land. Write a narrative to tell what happens.

Real-World Language Arts: Investigative Journalist

An investigative journalist investigates and reports news via print, TV, or the Internet. Many investigative journalists study journalism and communication arts. They must learn about reporting and writing. Additionally, an investigative journalist must study ethics, or moral values. His or her reporting should be free from prejudice or bias. Investigative journalists must also be able to use a variety of technology. Many journalists investigate and report on camera, but they also work behind the scenes. They edit and produce as well. If you're interested in a career in this field, you need to master the art of writing and editing as well as speaking.

Language Is Life

The assignments in language arts class are just like real life. If you can lend a listening ear, plan a party, learn a dance, or bake a batch of cookies, then you can tackle any language arts assignment. It's all about communication. Read to understand. Speak and write to express yourself. Remember that if you can communicate effectively and confidently, people will pay attention. An essay is no reason to break a sweat or chip a nail. You have what it takes to be a savvy student and rule language arts class!

ANSWER KEY

Chapter 1

Pop Quiz (page 11): Adjectives describe nouns (extra credit if you also wrote pronouns), and adverbs describe verbs.

Pop Quiz (page 15): compound sentence

Bonus Point (page 15): but

Learn the Language (pages 20–21):

1. simple

2. complex

3. compound-complex

4. compound

5. Answers will vary. Tip: A simple sentence has one independent clause.

6. Answers will vary. Tip: A compound sentence has two independent clauses joined by either a comma followed by a conjunction or a semicolon.

7. Answers will vary. Tip: A complex sentence has one independent clause and one subordinate clause.

Bonus points: Write it two ways. First use the subordinate clause at the beginning and include a comma. Then write it with the independent clause first and leave the comma out.

8. Answers will vary. Tip: Compound-complex sentences have at least three clauses—one subordinate and two independent.

Chapter 2

Pop Quiz (page 27): third person point of view

Learn the Language (page 33):

1. Answers will vary. Tip: The sequence of events should be events that involve the conflict. The conflict is the problem faced by the main character. The resolution is the solution to the problem, or the way the conflict is solved. The theme is what the character learns.

2. Answers will vary. Tip: Write your description based on how the character behaves, what he or she says, and what others say about him or her.

3. Answers will vary. Here are some samples:

Similes:

The bulldog was as mean as a school bully.

Her eyes were blue like sapphires.

The newborn chick was as soft as a cotton ball.

Metaphors:

He's a beast when he plays football.

My little sister turns into a monster when she doesn't get her way.

My neighbor is usually cranky, but when she talks to her kitten she becomes an adoring mother.

Chapter 3

Pop Quiz (page 37): You read nonfiction to gain information. You read literature (or fiction) to enjoy the plot and be entertained.

Commercial Break (page 39): Sample answer: Sparkle toothpaste claims to make your teeth their whitest. The evidence the company gives is two photos: before and after shots of the model who used the product for two weeks. While the model's teeth look whiter, one person's experience isn't enough proof to show the product works. It gets a C-.

Bonus Point (page 40): How-to directions

Make Your Own Photo Booth (pages 40–41):

(2) boas Context
(4) selfies Definition
(1) backdrop Example
(3) templates Restatement

Party Games (page 43):

1. How-to directions
2. Compare and contrast
3. Problem/solution

Chapter 4

Bonus Point (page 49): another
Pop Quiz (page 51): The purpose of an argument is to see if you can make a claim and prove it.

Learn the Language (page 58):

Give yourself one point for each item you did correctly.

_____ written as a story with clear beginning, middle, and end
_____ includes a conflict
_____ conflict is resolved at the end
_____ first-person point of view is used consistently throughout
_____ vivid, descriptive details are included
_____ story is interesting and exciting
_____ character changes or learns a lesson by the end (theme)
_____ paper is neat and has margins and a title
_____ story is broken into paragraphs
_____ capitalization and punctuation are correct throughout

If you scored 9 or 10, excellent! Got a 7 or 8? Pretty good. Only 6 or lower? Try again.

GLOSSARY

characterization (KARE-ick-ter-uh-ZAY-shun)—giving someone or something a quality or feature

clause (KLAWZ)—a group of words that includes a subject and a predicate

conflict (KON-flict)—a disagreement

dialogue (dy-UH-log)—the words spoken between two or more characters; in writing, dialogue is set off with quotation marks

fragment (FRAG-ment)—a word, phrase, or clause that is not a complete sentence

infer (in-FUR)—to draw a conclusion after considering all the facts

literature (LI-tur-uh-CHUR)—written work of fiction

part of speech (PART OF SPEECH)—a group of words that is one of adjective, adverb, noun, conjunction, interjection, preposition, pronoun, or verb

plot (PLOT)—the sequence of events that drives a story forward; the problems that the hero must resolve

prompt (PRAHMPT)—instruction that leads you to do something

point of view (POINT UV VYOO)—the way someone or something looks at or thinks about something

resolution (rez-uh-LOO-shun)—the point in literature when the conflict is worked out

text feature (TEXT FEE-chur)—words or visuals that appear in addition to the main text

theme (THEEM)—main idea that the story addresses, such as good versus evil or the importance of truth; a story can have more than one theme

tone (TONE)—a way of speaking or writing that shows a certain feeling or attitude

READ MORE

Fogarty, Mignon, and E. Haya. *Grammar Girl Presents the Ultimate Writing Guide for Students.* New York: St. Martin's Griffin. 2011.

Vickers, Rebecca. *Making Better Sentences: The Power of Structure and Meaning.* Chicago: Heinemann, 2014.

Vickers, Rebecca. *Punctuation and Spelling: Rules That Make Things Clear.* Chicago: Heinemann, 2014.

INTERNET SITES

FactHound offers a safe, fun way to find Internet sites related to this book. All of the sites on FactHound have been researched by our staff.

Here's all you do:

Visit *www.facthound.com*

Type in this code: 9781491407738

Check out projects, games and lots more at
www.capstonekids.com

INDEX

adjectives, 8, 10, 19
adverbs, 8, 10, 19
apostrophes, 17
argument, 4, 45, 49, 50, 51, 58

characters, 18, 23, 24, 28, 29, 30, 32, 33, 49, 55
characterization, 29
claims, 35, 42, 50
clauses, 12, 13, 14, 15, 16, 21
    independent, 12, 13, 14, 15, 21
    subordinate, 12, 13, 14, 15, 21
commas, 14, 15, 16, 17, 21
communication, 4, 19, 59
conclusions, 45, 46, 47, 49, 53
conflict, 23, 24, 26, 28, 31, 32, 33, 54, 55
conjunctions, 8, 11, 14, 17
contractions, 17

dashes, 16
dialogue, 18, 31, 54, 55

editing, 56, 59
evidence, 35, 42, 51
exclamation marks, 16
explanation, 45, 49, 52, 53, 54, 58

fragments, 13

grammar, 4, 6, 19, 43
graphic organizers, 47

idioms, 31
inferences, 26, 27

informational texts, 34, 35, 36, 37, 38, 40, 41, 42, 43
    cause and effect, 37
    chronology, 37
    compare and contrast, 37, 43
    how-to directions, 37, 43
    problem/solution, 37, 38, 43
interjections, 8, 11
items in a series, 17

language, 4, 6, 8, 16, 19
literature, 4, 22, 23, 29, 30

main idea, 35, 46, 47
metaphors, 31, 33

narrative, 45, 49, 54, 55, 58
nouns, 8, 9, 10

outlines, 47

parentheses, 16
parts of speech, 8, 11
periods, 16
plot, 23, 26, 31, 32, 33, 54
points of view, 24, 25, 26, 27, 54
    first person, 24, 27
    third person, 25, 27
possessives, 17
    plural, 17
predicate, 9, 19
prepositions, 8, 10
prewriting, 46, 51
prompts, 45, 46, 50, 53, 54, 58
pronouns, 8, 9, 24, 25

punctuation, 16, 17, 43

question marks, 16
quotations, 17, 35

research, 4
resolution, 28, 31, 32, 33, 49
revising, 56

scripts, 31
semicolons, 14, 16
sentences, 9, 10, 12, 13, 14, 15, 17, 19, 20, 21, 46, 47, 51
    complex, 14, 20, 21
    compound, 14, 17, 20, 21
    compound-complex, 15, 20, 21
    simple, 14, 20, 21
    topic, 51, 53
similes, 30, 31, 33
speaking, 4, 19
subjects, 9, 12, 13, 19

text features, 36, 42
theme, 28, 31, 32, 33
tone, 45, 47, 58
transitions, 45, 48, 49, 53, 55, 58

verbs, 8, 9, 10, 12, 13

writing, 4, 19, 31, 44, 45, 46, 47, 48, 49, 50, 51, 52, 53, 54, 55, 56, 57, 58